Dear Tom,

MAIDEN VOYAGE

HEATHER WELLS

It was a pleasure to meet you & thank you so much for buying a copy! Enjoy this book of poems.

From,
Heather Wells.

2nd Feb 2015

© Heather Wells 2014

Heather Wells has asserted her rights under the Copyright, Design and Patents Act, 1988, to be identified as the author of this work.

First published in 2014

Cover and layout design by Shane Ellis

SPONSORED BY
THE LONDON MAGAZINE

To my everything – Mum
In Memory – Dad
In Hope – Jonathan

CONTENTS

THE AWAKENING

Wretched Web	8
Premonition	9
Blood Cherry	10
Child of the Earth	11
Fallen Hope	13
Map Eyes	14
Curiosity	15
Impressionable	18
End of the Line	20

CEMETERIES OF LONDON

Hilly Highgate	22
The Old Moon	24
All Souls	25
Names of the Dead	27
Autumn Mottle	29
Hardy Tree	30

EYES SPANNING SEVEN GENERATIONS

Grandparent	32
Emil	33
Silence	34
Family Gathering	35
Ode to Memory	37
Selina	38
One Less Day	39

MISCELLANEOUS

Sacred Stones	42
Chiaroscuro	43
Companions of Conflict	44
Shake me up	45
Bloomsday	46
Shoreditch	48
Female Core	49
Love Bite	50
Moments	51
Spindly Fingers	52
Bruce Nauman	53
I Want to be Jane Eyre	54
Boxed-In	56
Winter Warmth	57
This Garden is a Marriage	58
When These Men Grow Up	59
Maiden Voyage	61
Epitaph	62

ANARCHY IN THE ATMOSPHERE

"My Body is a TV'ed Massacre"	64
Yesterday was a Gift	65
Letters	68
Hook, Line and Sinker	69
Dream, Wish and Reality	70
Queuing for Citizenship	73
Tribal	74
Novels	75
Jubilant!	76
Blue to Purple	79

THE AWAKENING

Wretched Web

A web of entanglements
invisible: soaked by day light.
Lace under the moonlight.
Powdered secrecy.

The cobweb's lace
covers each moon-struck face.
The web quivers, the wind trembles
each delicate spine
of chained net.

The web broken,
each wisp rekindled.

Premonition

Pain eeks onto the pillow.
Its faulty tap a lasting leak.
Distressed. Sleepless night.

Dying to sleep. Sleeping to die.
Dying to wake. Remove this
compressed band around my head.

Awake. I see your name.
Each letter stamped on skin.
Strange as spaghetti hoops.

Splash of wet fish. This is
conscious. They wriggle
cold all over you.

The mind numb, lingers.
The heart does not.

Sensing it just as much now
as I can the line of words
that read: I saw it coming.

Blood Cherry

Prick of the blood cherry.
Ravished.
You won the eye staring.
Inevitable.

Doleful deer. Fumbling legs.
Slips on sharp cruel ice.
Cuts thin watery skin.

Suckled to my breast.
I should have smothered you
there and then like Lady Macbeth.

Spasmic eyeballs
fucked into oblivion.

Cold ashamed Eve.
Rollercoaster drug swirls.
Mad as you.
'Sorry.' 'What?' 'Sorry.' 'Go.'

Sobering water runs
with hospital blood.

Glowing skin. Idle eyes
remain 'cocktailed'.
Sip ... and it's over.

Child of the Earth

I stare at my toes heavy-eyed under a blazing sun.
But I'm woken by the itchy grass as dry as my parched skin.
I seek out the boy with the dark eyes.
The caves of his eyes do not meet me back.
They seek out new pastures
laden with promises.

New day, new risen sun,
replenishes in the morning; seepage at night.
To ask the sun what it has seen in the day
is to ask what the sea has kept at bay.

Have I forgotten the worries of yesterday?
I have not. They appear to have forgotten you.

The sun is two motions. Awakes. Retires.
The seas exhale and inhale.
They never stop.
We all live and We all have to die.

I cannot live in the furnace sun,
nor can I withstand the ocean's depths.
Earth is my home.
Yet we are spinning inside a washing machine:
magnets at the centre of it all.
The cycle has finished, I am hung out to dry.

The sun stealthily robs me of moisture until I am desiccated.
Surrounded by buildings as unnatural as potions
there is no escape to the mountains.
And so I remain here
in the garden with the fountains.

Like little thoughts, birds swoon and take flight,
you hear the birdsong even out of sight.
'Innocence is something to applaud' I was told.
Now the words seem to have grown so old,
worn as a twisted branch that's knotted itself
wisely through times of downpour.

Déjà-vu stuns my world.
Suddenly all moments become one
in a psychedelic prism of fun.
The images soon disperse into the giddy face of a lake,
and those tremors ripple away for all our sake.

The orange outline where the sun lights up my feet
illuminates the skin to reveal fleshy pink blood-filled toes
vulnerably transparent as the delicate membrane of memory.

Dumbfounded by my own boredom
and gazing at my sun-kissed toes
something unseen has shifted
to align itself again with the universe.

Fallen Hope

Beacons of hope slope into quicksand
along with words that
crumble me into rubble.

Acidic truth. A need greater
more futile than my own.
Crystallised in a distant memory.

I'm left with the debris
you've thrown at me.

The base overwhelming need
for selfish love.
A dependent parasite
on ice cold blood.

Cruel, morbid frozen figures
letting the old breadwinner die
never having her children return.

But keeping out late at night
with yellow eyes, like the foxes they are.

Map Eyes

A life built up by books.
Stories not my own.
Gangsters. Red-blooded lives
on edge of this tender
world we temporarily live.

Idle long lie-ins.
Rotations in the room.
Life outside the window.
Crippling inner tomb.

Why bother to get out of bed today?
Still in pyjamas late noon on a sunny day.
Wasted on me, not them.

Walking nowhere. Thinking
everywhere. Getting nowhere.
Defeat. Just me and skeleton.

Inertia. Too afraid
to go get life. Disengaged.
Mopping up wet map eyes.

Curiosity

4pm –
lull of day.

You make a suggestion,
one I do not question.

Tart myself up for you,
on display on the tube.

Piccadilly, the arc
runs right through Finsbury Park.

Missed call from your name.
No longer a game.

Hooded eyes. Religion.
Flicker to the pigeons.

Like some strange bright warning
two police are yawning.

Focus on their faces.
Hear you quicken your pace.

You lock my lips with yours.
'You made the effort.' 'Course.'

You play it cool, low key.
We're both nervous, I see.

It's been more than a year.
Different now you're near.

That old thud in my chest.
Throat closing, and the rest.

Confident there's control.
Dally and loll.

Fruit swelters in windows.
Students puff, pout, pose.

Turning me on my heel.
In street you cop a feel.

You pull me in on rope.
Kiss sweet, minty, smoky.

Good Omens was the book.
Stop, take a look.

Door fifteen in my search.
You live next to a *church*?

The irony. Religion.
Ally Pally. Imagine.

Shimmy me up the stairs.
Strip leather jacket bare.

I wake to neon lights,
Obama speeches at night.

You. Outside the bubble
it wasn't so much trouble.

Impressionable

Why push yourself back into my life?
A letter under my door, except it was blank.

I adopted a passive role, while you were dominant.
The idea should have appalled me.
It didn't. It enthralled me.

That was until I saw you.
You looked jagged, jaded,
burnt-out.

You'd regressed, rather than progressed.
Become more of a lost boy,
certainly not a graduate to employ.

For years I placed you on a pedestal.
Admire the sheer ability: dare
affront anyone or anything.

Finsbury Park is not quite Highgate.
Nor is apathy as attractive as it once was.
You boy, have lost your charm.

Bold. Brazen with me.
Frisky. *We could go for a drink,*
but I'd just stare at your tits all night.

I remember it all.
Old black and white movie.
I remember it all in black and white.
A Ballard character sat on the floor.
Rough and wild. On the edge
of modern civilised society.
Close to collapse
in a state of baboonery.
Beating your chest.
Nurse to a sick infantile.

Then there was *that* face.
What was in *that* face?
A disturbed yet peaceful face.
Beautifully vulnerable.
Dangerous to worship.
Surely, none can resist *that* face.
Disbelieving eyes as I look at *that* face
which for me, at that moment in time
holds gold dust.
I take it as a good omen,
and turn my back.
Heavy with the image of *that* face.

End of the Line

Four of the five senses have been stripped;
Our voices solemnly left dancing around the bonfire.
I hear you, and imagine to see you
Your terrible fragile sigh can reach me.
But your breath lingers, and not on me.
Our voices become the master of all trades,
we use words to entice, fragments of desire.
Your voice reacts on me like aspirin to water
but so much grander the reaction would be if I had
your eyes, your smell, your hands, your mouth,
your body as well as your voice.

CEMETERIES OF LONDON

Hilly Highgate

Graveyard keepers warn us in the still courtyard:
"There are no straight paths in the whole of the West Cemetery."
A bird's-eye view shows life's twisted turns and crooked paths,
Litvinenko's severed pillar: symbol of a life cut short.

Attempts to tame what is already wild, as the graves
lie deranged. A family vault guarded by canons disarmed.
Life meets death in the daylight,
yet sinister shadows lurk in corners for nightfall.

Decayed bark befriends evergreen ivy.
It's a strangely alive place.
Trees extend their arms to our beating hearts on the woodchip
before we pass through Egyptian Avenue tombs.
Ventilation holes breathe on us an anointment before
we tread on holy ground in the circle of Lebanon.

The Cedar of Lebanon droops its frazzled barnet over the
yoghurt-coloured slabs, tiresomely protecting a hierarchy.
The backdrop of St Michael's silhouette where Coleridge is lain
imposes the cemetery. The Napoleon of Crime is allotted
the smallest of patches as Sherlock's arch enemy – Moriarty.

Siddal is interred with the Rossetti's, but not her Dante,
his dug-up devotions of lyricism adorned in her fiery hair.
Above, the trees exhale violently. A sleeping angel is alert –
its body flung onto stone awaiting a second coming.

A photograph captured the scene shows the angel watching me,
its eyes burning the back of my head.

The Old Moon

Our graveyard in moonlight.
Is anything more inspired?
Spectral grey hub of souls,
icy-carved headstones, marble statues
and angels safeguarding the dead.
Sight of a few withered flowers.
Walking alive through decay and death,
my soul cannot resist leaping in its pocket:
'let me lay down in peace!'
But it contradicts itself:
stubbornly thumps louder to assert
its blood life force –
it will not be drained, yet.
The night isn't frightening or chilling
but calm and hot as blood.
The deafening silence of a stillborn.
Gone is the pigment of your eyes, buried
for only the coffin lid to gaze upon
the image of the living is gone.
We only feel them as they
reach out to us in the grass.

All Souls

The cemetery itself dies. Lack of funding.
But flowers will grow anywhere.
Even on tops of chapels.
Three famed dead bodies lie here:
Thackeray, Brunel and Trollope
as pigeons nest in oval holes of a mausoleum.
The path forks as if it'd been tampered.
In the cemetery office a red-faced man offers us a map
and fervently marks the three graves on the plot's lap.
"Wilkie Collins is also here" he says.
We tell him we've just come from Brompton.
Proudly he speaks of his ancestor buried there
 – by the name of Fortune.
"This is the man recognised for introducing
tea plants from China to India" he tells us.
We look for Isambard Kindgom Brunel:
his name won't go unnoticed, his tomb would.
The man who gave us Clifton suspension bridge
and The Great Western Railway
takes no glory after death.
Thackeray is nearby.

Treading on lumpy mounts of grass
around graves just to find an inscription,
a clue to tell me where he is in this maze.
In surprise we find him next to red-brick,
a lone candle sits on his tomb.
His name is completely eroded –
poor Thackeray. His grave is so forlorn.
Onto Trollope:
'Into thy hand I commit my spirit'
If it were not so short, I should say:
'What a load of Trollope!'
Author of *Woman in White*
my eyes cannot see Collins grave in sight
mysterious as the night-light.
All is so quiet.

Names of the Dead

Brompton – formally Westminster
nears the road. Car fumes
contaminate sacred ground
and stealthily hover by cemetery bars.

Ravens dark, shiny as black tar
roam the grounds primitively.
As cemetery keepers they heavily flutter
thick wings brazenly treading gravestones.

Wild expanse of long grass speckled with sweet peas.
Grasshoppers or crickets play their consistent note
hidden in the overgrown, shadowed by cool tomb stones.

Beatrix Potter borrowed names of the dead from here:
Peter Rabbett, Jeremiah Fisher, Mr Nutkins.
So I too borrowed a few names
delicately placing them in my mind's silk pocket.

Charlotte Leishman, William Ayrton
and cherishing the strong surnames:
Waples, Ellis and Leggett.

The wonderful thoroughfare
as cyclist's glisten in and out of light
caught in the spokes of their wheels.

Children play unfazed.
The drunkard scratches his head
unkempt as his surroundings.

A woman weeps for a recent loss.
A policeman at the gate lacks force in a place like this.
An impressive colonnade at the centre
the most dramatic place to stage a play.

The cemetery marks the dwelling place
of honourable Emmeline Pankhurst,
though the grave goes unnoticed for most
unlike her violent death.
A few pale pink roses left
at her side an old oak tree.

Autumn Mottle

Misty stone-stepped pathway
on corner's edge,
kingdom of the dead.

Tombs lay sunk, arrayed like junk.
Sea of 200,000 souls
in an unconsecrated hole.

Autumn mottle
dimly dampened
dew in a bottle.

Victorian garden cemetery.
You find monument
with skeletal plant entwined.

An arboretum tree
has fallen to its knee.

Abney, the daughter park of
Bunhill, or Bone hill
scatters the dead, dandelions bled.

Hardy Tree

The petrol-smoked hum of the city
surrounds St Pancras Old Churchyard.
Its steps glorify the feet of those who ascend
and the newlyweds who descend.

The light of the community spirit dares to dance
upon headstones. Goodwill basks in the sun.
It delights on windswept wavy branches held high,
as it peers out onto industrial cranes ever lofty.

The brotherhood of death, gravestone slabs
in rows and rows so on and so on ...
The meek winding path bears the last few strides
of pilgrimage unto The Hardy Tree.

Here, less lean, more cluster, the shoots of graves
become the army of the ash tree.
The ash himself has borne life to it,
nutrients zapped by the suckling force of spirits.

EYES SPANNING SEVEN GENERATIONS

Grandparent

Eyes spanning seven generations,
fiery eyes, melting the mind
behind them. Loose gums. Sucked cheeks.
A gabble of gibberish German.

She licks hot-choc off a finger
which she circles the mug's innard.
She used to be so reserved,
grandmotherly. Now she's a jokester
adrift on a fantasy path.

If she could she'd take you round
the garden again. The sun's a killer.
It shrivels the shrivelled skin.

The best thing is watch a baby
being pushed around the place
oblivious to her adventure,
in destructive, bony body, softing mind.

Emil

Emil, gone, scattered.
You are the hole in my heart.
Emil has left his boots by the door
and he didn't come back.
I know I pray too much.

Silence

We stand in silence.
The trees drip.
Ravens warn each other
that we are hard by.

The gift of the fall
of a leaf, rather early.
It wants to make contact, to be
a confirmation.

The taking of photos.
Sacrilege, in a way.
Eleven years on
we have moved on.

Now we can look
around us, or at each other,
or no where.
There is no where to hide,
no special place to go.

We can go where we want.
It no longer matters.

Family Gathering

The birthday girl greets us
heeled, black velvet,
Gothic on a summer's day.

The familiar family look strange.
Time has made a small change.
A baby girl ballooned into a child
and my eyes are seeing for the first time.

A spread of meat cools on a paper plate.
A bright windy BBQ day.
Chargrilled sweetcorn and
slimy courgette fingers.

Rotating bums on seats.
Children drinking on their feet,
re-filling coke in a cup.

Birthday girl's string of photos
mark the eighteenth occasion.
Grinning, youthful faces stuck to the fence.

Singing happy birthday
champagne in plastic cups
and sickly coloured icing.

An oral celebration:
"She is the best of her dad and her mum"
branded a fighter in adversity.

A tearful birthday girl
who feels loved and emotional
... this is a social after all.

Ode to Memory

It came from no-where
So can I blow it back to nowhere?
It's just that every time I do,
It bounces back and hits me in the face
A car crash –
Shock as it hits my windscreen,
Which, I thought could handle the force.

Selina

Born in May
on the twenty-fourth day.
Pure pink blossom
warmed butterfly wings
flitting.

Sally, her name means *Princess*.
Her shawl draped in lavender.
She pours love into food parcels.
Wholesome as anzacs, oatcakes, flapjacks,
Bara brith, sealed with a kiss.

Blue eyes talk to me in the garden,
meadow-yellow locks from childhood
grace her silver-hair.

Rowan kidsilk-haze illuminates
a whisper of wool, leaving its
icy trail on her lacy shawl.

Without you, the stratosphere cracks.

One Less Day

One less day
or one more day lived
depending what mood I'm in.

Cry just at the thought.
Sometimes I get so hysterical
my scream is silenced.

Visions I won't be able to move –
paralysed I will sit in my chair
(not yours)
and stare blankly for days.
Light, then night
falling on my face.

I fear my own death,
we will die the same day
and life will go on.

I will talk to the walls
like you do now
when I'm away.

The dull silence will ache.
Your face will become a mirage.
Your voice an archaic note
on a piano no longer in use.
To play it taps a bruise.

These things I have left of you:
the ever blurring face
and detached voice
float in an ever-growing void.

Attachment is lost.
My closest
becomes my most estranged.
And I will not rest
until my pain is pulled
when I join whence I began.

MISCELLANEOUS

Sacred Stones

High-walled Abbey gardens,
ravens perch and defend.

Stony ruins imitate shapes
unseen by long dead monks.

Frozen roses
swampy pond weeds.

St Edmundsbury heralds its gem
less boastful than an emerald.

The hammerbeam roof exalts
above the Cathedral floor.

In the nave I see you stand at the high-altar,
Father with son, reverent scene –

Sears the sacred
onto constant memory.

The vulnerable son in awe
senses the pillars present.

Rooted over this ground
where a mark of history is felt.

Chiaroscuro

You stand at the door,
feet snug in socks.
Clinging to carpet:
moss upon the sea-faced rock.

Step back. Cobbled ground,
uneven as my boot heel
worn down.
My sweeping arm a wave.

Firmly the door closes.
Tentatively I shut the porch.
Our faces held in the night
under torchlight.

Breathing evening exhales
deeply, damply as the moon
softy shines on slabs of shabby stone,
as a new chiaroscuro grows.

Grey formless
spirits of shadow pass us.
Granular memories disperse
like childhood friends.

Companions of Conflict

Marching towards a front line,
the unmarked generation.
Somnolent fumbling with their hands
the space in front of them.
Segmented into stitched pockets
loaded with ear-muffs clogged.
Impersonal, distant voices,
brains blotted. The jargon of other's lives:
the status, boasts, seemingly knowing.
The acting generation
tuned into an alter-machine.
The companions of conflict
desensitizing our compassion and
fighting for our attentions.

Shake me up

Shake me up
with maddening love.
Pump blood to the exterior of the skin.
A premonition of what it might be
alive and full of vitality.

Wasted on my own.
Cold knuckles
gripping the pen as I write.
My company kept and the tainted ideas
longing for a new method of breathing.
A stranger, turned friend
changing the rhythms in your feet
to follow a different beat.

I'm a moth waiting to shed its
dusty wings,
heavy.
Save my bored and dissatisfied soul
before I stagnate into a frozen egg.

Bloomsday

I
Cross-legged, purling
soft pale pink cotton.
The DAB broadcasts itself.
It is Bloomsday.
I stop my day, ask it to listen.

Follow the Dublin wanderer:
as Leopold eats his giblets
as Stephen Dedalus theorises Shakespeare
as Blazes Boylan threatens Bloom's interior.

Andrew Scott's voice:
low lilt of the Irish tongue –
soft, menacing.
Its breathy sound sings a hypnotic song.
I mistake it for a blanket, when it's a hissing snake.
In between readings, I resume my life.

I book train tickets to Seascale.
Lunchtime. German hotdogs in a white flaky bun.
I print our travel itinerary to Dublin.
Precious minutes gone
on a tiresome credit card application.
I've missed the 2.30pm slot.
I tune in mid-flow
but am lost on the Dublin map.

I start to compare my day
with Bloom's in the present past.
He has walks to the post-office. Real butcher's meat.
Letters slid in pockets, converse with neighbours.
He has walking and purpose and contact – real contact.
I have computer screens, processed meat, a digital world
of distant people, a click away.

II

At 4.20pm I have a new direction.
It leads to a destination
that is a dead-end,
except into an investigation
that will feed my own elation.
To sum it up would be wordy as a dissertation.

My day overtakes Bloomsday.
A curious event, as fierce as an awakening.
The day has transformed
from ordinary to extraordinary.
The day has put on its cloak.
I dare not think.
For me, this could put me on the brink.
Quickly – before I blink.

Shoreditch

West to East London,
there are garments hanging
from high-rise balconies
ghost figures watching the track lines
as empty trains go by.

Fluorescent plastic heels totter,
waves of indie bands animate life
making me feel, oh so lonely
in my green mac – as I wait
under the brutal throttled sky
above the flyover.

Female Core

Willowy Pre-Raphaelite,
Guinness in hand.
Rose plucked and placed
between two male thorns.

Brazilian prostitutes,
handed blooms of beauty
not the greasy *real*
crumpled in sweaty palms.

Female core, hard
as coconut shell,
inside clear water runs.
Fluid. Incandescent.
Phosphorescent.

If it were to bleed
milk should turn claret.
Tears would drown her
in a lonely lily pond.

Love Bite

Love bites.
One on each cheek.
Purplish-bluish broccoli
florets. Burst blood vessels.
A moment of lust
boldly on my face.
Far too public.
Try to cover the blemish
with tan foundation
over cell tissue.
Stubbornly they still show
underneath.
I am marked, dirtied
by a cluster of veined-speckles.
I feel forsaken.
They don't hold tenderness.
It obscures the face as
a branch to the moon
making it less beautiful
and more spiky.
Love bites and bruises
even these are temporary.

Moments

Happiness
doesn't
last
for
a
long time
But
I
will
have it
when its
due to
me
I will
take what is
rightfully
mine.

It is easier when time is not linear,
but instead is a mass of fluttered moments.

Spindly Fingers

Conductor's hand rise and fall –
a free-floating maple leaf,
yet attached to a limb as conducive
as the wind blowing seeds.

Violin lines point to the heavens in unison,
upright, waiting for anointment –
the signal whispers in my tentative ear,
not curtailing: it *will* be alright.

A ruby goddess seizes the grand
piano, tantalises the keys.
Energy surges through the strong spine –
drawn out in exorcism.

Sublime found in an academy
like one of many halls in *Anna Karenina*.
A French horn to be played by a chiseled face
as desire seeps amid wild musical notes.

Bruce Nauman

Pause in Bruce Nauman's dark space
in the light White Cube.
Competing with Damien Hirst.
Painted parrots. Japanese flowers.
Scissors doing the splits.
Rubber foetuses in jars.
Yours is colourless in contrast.

Yet, in your rooms
my footsteps won't move fast,
for *you've* built something to last.
Black and white videos replay.
Flickers on susceptible membrane.
A single man. Few sequential movements.
Beckettian.

Cocooned in your exhibition space.
Walls and dim-light make me safe.
In odd rhythmic sounds I bathe.
The whine of the discordant violin,
with the hollow ping-pong ball.
Standing before you as you move:
I can feel you behind me, to the side of me,
pulsating in my dull still movement.

I Want to be Jane Eyre

I want to be Jane Eyre
who caresses the blind eye of Rochester.

I want to be Helen Graham
her eyes so clear and full of soul.
Standing for reformation and goodness,
paintbrush in hand.

I want to be Tess of the D'Urbervilles
whose innocence should be applauded.

I want to be Mary Yellan
who should've been born a man.
Fearless and free to roam the heather
bareback riding with Jem Merlyn.

I want to be Mai Kirwan
her lovely wedding dress like white seaweed
romantically in the rain
with her lover Jack McNulty.

I want to be Ursula Brangwen
who struggles but fights
to be herself
and is given a rainbow.

I want to be Catherine Earnshaw
passionate and wild.
One of the few believers
that romantic love is eternal.

An orphan, outcast, victim,
strong, unstable,
independent, and wild woman.
These are the heroines that haunt me.

Boxed-In

Boxed-in, dim-lit, and air-less.
Play a game of musical chairs
where sitting equals safety.
Unyielding brittle plastic chairs,
uncomfortable as I feel.

I grip my scarf so hard it hurts
and chew my milky white malleable nails.
The shabby, dishevelled people,
misfits of society worn out like rag dolls.

As I seek refuge in the brutally clinical room,
there in the seat ahead of me is a huge white
arse-crack, I giggle like a schoolchild.
I feel ok for a moment.

Oh, God forbid the talk starts
and the thudding returns:
it bruises the casement of my ribs,
it will not rest.

To disarm it I focus on the steeple
outside of the high-rise room,
and I hear the trams go by
and wish I were outside walking.

Winter Warmth

Weather-beaten. Sodden.
In the street I ogle.
Kith and kin gather.
Sleet falls, pitter-patter.

Ochre-glow cavern
bustling as a park tavern.
Smell of nut roast
and candle smoke, I imagine.

The clink of clay-spun mugs
that spill on sheepskin rugs.
Angelic music permeates,
entwines itself like ivy.

Hesitance lingers on my breath,
as mist loiters on the wreath.
The brass knocker glares.
All I do is stare.

This Garden is a Marriage

This garden is a marriage.
One between beauty and heaven,
resounding in truth.
Large solid trees, a canopy overhead
like the shrouded veil.

Alone, yet thinking of everyone else,
unable to absorb my thoughts.
Waiting for an epiphany to spring on me
but it seems to tease me
and I am none the wiser.

Restless to share my pleasure
in the warm sun with another,
but unload my chaos too.
Incapable of sitting alone
with misery and happiness.

Reluctant to leave the bench
in case the revelation comes.
I pine for a grain that will nourish me,
help me to breathe again
in my new-found space.

When These Men Grow Up

Spat out.
No.
That'd imply I've
been chewed up,
minced up, then
spewed out.

But I haven't.
No-one's spat me out.
They haven't harmed me,
but it's what they don't do
that pains me.

When these men grow up
I will be an old woman.

Where are all the men?
Where are all the men.

Weak, pitiful men
lacking lustre.

Oh how I long for
the change – in others.

These thirsty men
who take everything
like a boozer to his drink.
Guzzling it down,
rousing red rosy cheeks
while our pale pallor
lingers on tear-stained skin.

Oh I could wring them,
squeeze the excess liquid from them.

When all is quiet
an hour late
and clouds breathe
past the curtained windows
you will still see us
waiting on a change of wind.
The corpse hand dangling down.

Maiden Voyage

Preserved ghost ship. Vast ocean,
slowly shifting on top of silt.
Underwater museum, unveiled by sonar.
Grave corpse of a bride
wedded to shores of New York City.

Untamed iceberg punctures vessel,
stranded on moonless night.
Lost to a minefield grey sea.
The poisonous sky covers it.

Mothers, children first.
Panic and howling,
the stern rises up bellowing.

They drop as pins
into the icy ocean
to join the other brave faced water-lilies
bobbing on its surface.

Captain takes on a new expression
as he looks, down at his warped ship.
Where class no longer matters.

Epitaph

The distant shores
are not so distant.

They were forever fast approaching
but we didn't worry about them.

We marooned on islands instead
forgetting the bigger picture.

Ripples in the water
but you can't spend too long on an island.

You look overseas.
What do you find?

One big expanse,
never sure of the currents
but one thing:
the tide always carries you.

My end is not violent.
The sea did not drown me.
It carried me beyond what we know.

ANARCHY IN THE ATMOSPHERE

"My Body is a TV'ed Massacre"

"My body is a TV'ed massacre."
Those words thread and squirm
under my skin.
Shrill voice. Unsettling.

The poem is her antibody.
Words wreak wrath.
They'll wilt if idle.
This cruel crisis seeps deep.
Irate, yet not wanting to hate.

Desperate beating of her chest,
such warmth in brutality's ugly cave.
Longing for an ignorant ear to yield.

Chronic ache for fair freedom.
Irrational. Bloodied.
Foul-smelling scenes
centuries have endured.

You teach life, preaching amidst the temples
and ruins; an olive branch for peace and not victory.

Words inspired by Rafeef Ziadah

Yesterday was a Gift

Yesterday was a gift.
Rendezvous at the foot
of the one-handed adulterer.
What a pair we make. In our leathers.
Tentative hug, keen eye.

A sober conversation
with sips of coffee.
Shot of espresso for him.
Together at the art gallery
we are visually illiterate.

Hungry stomachs lead us.
I'll order vegetarian in respect.
We cheer ourselves with toffee-flavoured
Innis & Gunn and Belgian Vedett.

Discourse runs on fluid:
beer lines fall, refill.
We pay. We leave. Walk and smoke.
Watch an angry cyclist provoke.

We walk London by night.
Wonder at how many stop, look:
the ever-changing skyline.

Share a cigarette by the Golden Hind,
drunkenly mapping scenes of boarding
the ship, breaking out the port.

Happiness. Hold that thought.
Inhale intoxication.

Firmly he grabs my hand.
We leap into the Old Thameside Inn,
a warm hub of drinking and merriment.

I choose us a Blue Moon.
Leather against leather.
He says to me: 'You look sad.'
I reassure him it is my look.
I cannot help it. God forbid
he'd think it's the time I spend with him
(but I don't tell him this second thing).

The Blue Moon doesn't live up.
Its orangey sweetness sickens.
We knock the beer and it erupts
into a heap of slosh and glass.
My shoe crunches it against the
hard cold stone floor.
Naughty, but good children.
We leap away to another corner.

Nerve endings numb,
but we anticipate the kiss.
Prolong it out in a dance.

Letters

You suck on roll-ups. Slurp on coffee.
Brazen with alcohol. Beer and whiskey
Your cushioned life, an aura of
mist and perfume. Swerving the
crisp biting cold in which reality lies.
If it's not in bed you lie, you transport
into Kafka's fantasy lands,
or Lawrence's eroticism,
or the strategic *Das Kapital.*
You live inside your brain.
Rudely awakened by sharp pain
in your bent back, after hours
lost to a binded book.
You like the bird cage kept
closely, under the skin of my chest.
The fragility of it.
If you were to thrash it, should frighten you.
Disarm you. Alarmingly seduce you.
Your shoulder blades are magnetic.
Their strength is seductive.
I grip them, pulling you down onto me.
Solid. But tender tissues when pulled
or strained shall erupt – they are
as fragile as my skin covered bird cage.

Hook, Line and Sinker

Love's fool thrown into a seemingly smooth lake.
Unawares of the rippling undertones
as little fishy dances; I am your bait.
Enflamed and engulfed by thoughts of you
If you break my heart I'll have you to sue.
Not only will break mine, you'll break mama's too.
What seems to me as something fated,
yet somehow it appears already tainted
and happened before we even dated.
My dear, I've learnt that I must take this slow
even though I don't want it to be so.
And the heart is already hit by cupids bow.

Dream, Wish and Reality

I dreamt a dream
so vivid and so glass-like.
Sharp at the edges,
clear to look into
but once broken,
never replaced.

You were the main
character in the dream.
Our sub-plot became reality,
slowly the chess-pieces
were setting themselves up
for check-mate.

Slowly, surely, strategically,
glimpses of the place we'd reach,
the lives we'd live,
the lifestyle we'd wear.
Abruptly slashed on my life supply.

No love, except the flame that shirks
weary, broken and crucified
under the spotlight.
There is only the suffering remainder
of what it is to love,
and how much of ourselves we lose.

To hibernate I must go,
but love tugs at my fingers,
painful on each joint:
I must go on,
forty winks and I must resume.

The anger will come later,
the bitterness in sly comments
the hardness to my exterior
just in case it happens again.
But it won't, at least not like this.

Perhaps our bodies grow another layer
each time the heart is wrenched
until its weight lays heavy
sinking us into saggy, wrinkly old
skin and bones.

Atoms drop on my thinking space.
Nerve endings in high alert,
raw to touch.
The pain travels downward
into the throbbing black cave of a heart
fighting for its right.

Inner chaos while around there is
deadening silence.
Withdrawn and hostile, the sobs are
my only contact with the real world.

The feelings I felt with you
were like trying on a new shoe.
It fitted, it was comfy and looked good.
But you never gave it a chance to mould.
You abruptly threw me off and left me to go back
to my old worn-in shoes, so moulded
that they can never be reset.

Should I throw them?
Or should I get used to how they feel again?
It really is a hard decision, because a pair
of shoes carry you through this life –
which is why I think that
the barefoot have got it sorted.

Queuing for Citizenship

Beckett House sounds homely, literary, Irish.
But on St Thomas Street, postcode SE1,
beside the hospital where the Rastaman sits
tucked in newspaper, foreign nationals queue.
A cluster on a street corner under the Shard.

Clutter spills on the road. Babies, buggies, baggage.
Identity papers, sodden spliffs propped up by
supporting mouths. Silence lingers, the city stirs.
Displaced into our country's open arms,
yet those arms seem to do more harm.

Shyness overcomes me passing hostile strangers.
Or did I invent their unfriendliness?
Pity penetrates my eyes that shirk away. *Why?*
Embarrassed, their sight a discomfort.
My conscience. Guilty of what? A lot, and not.

Citizenship I never had to queue for
in all weathers. I never even had to ask.
I've not fled my country.
But I welcome you here.
I don't have the dialogue to say this,
so I do not respond,
but bury it and carry on.

Tribal

We live our lives a den of matchsticks,
ignition at the ready, flames at the call.
Easily assembled, quick to fall.

Walking in on a new era,
retreading on dust blown away
and settled again.

Stepping with effervescence
into the gleam edge of future –
ready to nurture its distant pastures.

A mockery of the unforeseen.
The rainbow parachute snagged
on twisted twigs on the outreaching arm
of a disfigured tree.

The wooden, rotten tree
lies at the bottom of the ranch,
its tentacle roots ever-branching.

Novels

Hemingway, Nabokov, Hermann Hesse.
Favourite novelists of the men I love.

Decision looms. Shadow of a bow,
or a curtsy.
The novels, trapped fantasies.
Decision grows.

Heel to foot, I am connected
to the world, aligned to your
spoken word.

These men don't know
what these women are willing to show.

Man by definition has no womb
once mocked a woman's ambition
to give birth, then go to the tomb.

This woman knows not what she,
or any other woman declare for her life,
except that in all her strife
she'll soar as high as the night.

Jubilant!

Relaxed in your company
as the roamer roams the little streets
as the rambler rambles the moor
as the rower rows the boat.

We discuss royalty over triangles of pizza.
Asked by the man behind the counter
whether the blue or red wire is live.

Plunged deep in conversation,
we talk elitism. It turns into
an embedded paragraph, with a fenced-in
disagreement on marriage.

I struggle to scramble
coherent words like the pieces
on our scrabble board, like the
seven letter word 'stalled.'

I choose an Arvo Pärt CD,
drowsily it plays. We watch
the Great British Menu on the sofa
and lick caramel off spoons.

We sleep as two cocoons
lying flat out on our backs.
My shivering knee juts
into your side – other than that,
we do not touch.

We snooze like alarm clocks,
the Jubilee is upon us,
the Queen is hot on the tongue
and I am with an anarchist.

I shower and lace myself with
a robe that feels like decency.
Groom in front of you, knowing
I am being freely watched.

You fetch coffee.
Still in my underwear –
'kinky' you say.
Change into an English floral dress.
You compliment it.

We traipse down into town.
Agree to disagree re. the Jubilee.
Shake on it. Smash up some things,
you joke. I suggest you try your first cream tea.

We amble to the Contemporary, I see
hair that ripples long as the ocean bed.
A Mika Rottenberg film display

sharing the same space where
these long haired maids and their cows move.
Women devoid of any commerce.
Just sea-hair and cotton white dresses.
The beautiful eye blinks through wooden panels.

A bulbous nosed man sneezes out
raw red and white cartilage-boned meat,
a rabbit and then a light bulb.
I flinch as the products of his nose
hit the table surface,
where his coral painted toenails
curl and unfurl.

A fat black woman holds a lump of dough
as sweat drips down her bison sized thigh.
In a stifled working factory that
stinks the way nail varnish does.

Leaving. A Tokyo 18% at Brewdog.
Iodine excess trickling down
our sophisticated throats,
the night had promise.

You notice the look on my face
so we skip and we jump to keep warm in the rain
picking up the pace in the hovering lane,
a pale ale in a church pub.

Blue to Purple

Your mark on me fades
from blue to purple.
Ghastly looking,
but a healing bruise.

My pride discoloured.
Self-esteem squashed fruit pulp.
Photosensitive to you,
shirking from your unkind spotlight.

My dreams. My kindness.
My time. My sex.

Reluctant to write about you.
The time's come. It's resurrected
what I thought was numb.

No need to regurgitate,
this would be a sorry state.
Your words came all too late,
in a perverse way this paves our fate.

You won't be recalled as a legend,
though there are few that do.

And I hoped I was bound to one
like Juliet to her sun.
You took away all our fun,
your magic stopped being spun.

Undeserving of my words.
You gave me far too many, far too few.
I don't believe you: 'we are as free as birds.'
I may've been at your church
but I was at my own pew.

Today it dawned on me that our involvement
whilst I'll continue to keep it at bay
is as bedraggled as a rag soaked in salty tears.

To the sea it's tossed, frothing at the mouth.
Your memory of my youthful body,
your behaviour shamelessly uncouth,
drowned and endlessly thrashing against the rocks.

ACKNOWLEDGEMENTS

Thank you to everyone at *The London Magazine*
and all of its associates, in particular
Steven O'Brien and Grey Gowrie for their attention
and editing of the manuscript.

Many thanks to Richard Foreman for his invaluable advice
and to Amy Durant for all her help and guidance.

Special thanks to Shane Ellis for all of the design work
and his persistent encouragement that helped me
create a first collection to be proud of.

Thanks to all my family and friends.

Thanks also to all those who I have written about –
you know who you are.

Printed in Great Britain
by Amazon.co.uk, Ltd.,
Marston Gate.